ADAPTIVE INTELLIGENCE

It Is How You React to Situations and Conversations in Life That Defines Everything

ROHAN KAPUR

INDIA · SINGAPORE · MALAYSIA

Copyright © Rohan Kapur 2024
All Rights Reserved.

ISBN 979-8-89610-360-8

This book has been published with all efforts taken to make the material error-free after the consent of the author. However, the author and the publisher do not assume and hereby disclaim any liability to any party for any loss, damage, or disruption caused by errors or omissions, whether such errors or omissions result from negligence, accident, or any other cause.

While every effort has been made to avoid any mistake or omission, this publication is being sold on the condition and understanding that neither the author nor the publishers or printers would be liable in any manner to any person by reason of any mistake or omission in this publication or for any action taken or omitted to be taken or advice rendered or accepted on the basis of this work. For any defect in printing or binding the publishers will be liable only to replace the defective copy by another copy of this work then available.

Dedication

First of all, I want to thank myself first for being able to go through so much on my own and still find time to write this book, haha.

Jokes apart, I wouldn't be capable enough to write this if I wasn't born to my parents - Yogesh Kapur and Jyoti Kapur.

They invested in my education and experiences early on, and it's from those experiences that I've drawn inspiration for this book.

I wasn't smart enough to choose which school to go to when I was young and it was their choice that set the trajectory. When I wanted to study abroad it was their support that allowed my hard work to bear fruit.

Today, after living the majority of my adult life with them and seeing them navigate family, work, and life in general has given me a driver's seat view of how life is in "real" life and not in "reel" life.

Dedication

Instead of being frustrated about giving up my independence in the USA, I have enjoyed every single minute of living with them - sharing my professional highs and personal lows.

Also, saving on rent is an additional bonus.

I can never ever repay what they have provided for me, and this book is a small dedication from my side to them.

Lastly, Shreya, the reason we are where we are today is because of how both of us have **"adapted"** in our relationship. So thank you for always cheering me on from the sidelines, even on the days when life wasn't easy for you personally.

P.s. The most precious commodity in this world is time and I am glad I realised this **very** early on in my life, so along with chasing money, try to give that to whoever matters in your life in whatever way possible, in the end you will end up being way richer than a lot of people.

Why I wrote this?

The idea for this book has been with me for a very long time. I finalised the name when I was applying to ISB for an MBA in 2020.

The inspiration for the name came to me while working on my SOP for the college. While writing it I realised that throughout my journey, I've adapted to the circumstances I've been put in.

Rather than playing the victim card (well, sometimes I did, you can ask my mom!) I always managed to find a way back at school, at work, or discover my next opportunity.

This made me realise that the famous saying "life is 10% of what happens to you and 90% of how you react to it" is true. You'll never be able to plan the ideal career path, find the ideal life partner, the ideal family setting, and the ideal financial stability.

You need to be intelligent enough to be a realist and understand your current situation and how to make the best of it.

Why I wrote this?

This book is for people to remind them that being adaptable is not only limited to entrepreneurship or your professional life. To survive and be the best version of yourself, you need to face challenges head-on. Be less emotional and more solution oriented.

Being emotional is not bad, but having control over your emotions is necessary. When we feel an intense rush of emotion, it's our cue to take a break and not react. Sadly, we do the opposite.

Through this book, I'll cover instances in my life (professionally and personally) where I had to change my plans multiple times to reach where I am today.

From dreaming of being an architect, pivoting to studying Management Information Systems, becoming a part-time dishwasher, working full-time in data quality assurance to eventually falling in love with sales, and launching a startup whose bread and butter involves writing. The only thing that kept me going was adaptability.

On the personal front, today I'm **not** surrounded by a lot of people I thought would never leave my side. So I'll cover how the quality of being adaptable helps you navigate

Why I wrote this?

interpersonal relationships (be it a heartbreak or general disappointment with someone).

Because as life progresses you realise that you will be disappointed by others a lot. And being adaptable helps you not depend on others for your entire happiness. It helps you become comfortable with being alone (not lonely) and away from drama and focus on how you can evolve into the best version of yourself.

So in case you do end up facing disappointment, it's probably because of your own actions. And in order to overcome that disappointment, you end up improving yourself and becoming a better person.

Contents

Dedication   *3*

Why I wrote this?   *5*

Chapter 1	Adaptability	11
Chapter 2	Rejection is Redirection	18
Chapter 3	The Power of Pivot	26
Chapter 4	Looking Beyond Yourself	34
Chapter 5	The Power of Perspective	38
Chapter 6	Embracing Uncertainty	43
Chapter 7	The Flexible Mind	46
Chapter 8	Navigating the Unknown	50

Notes Page   *53*

Chapter 1

Adaptability

"Happiness is contentment"

Below was the first writing piece I ever wrote for **myself**, not for any English class, competitive exam, or assignment. I remember messaging my mom about it.

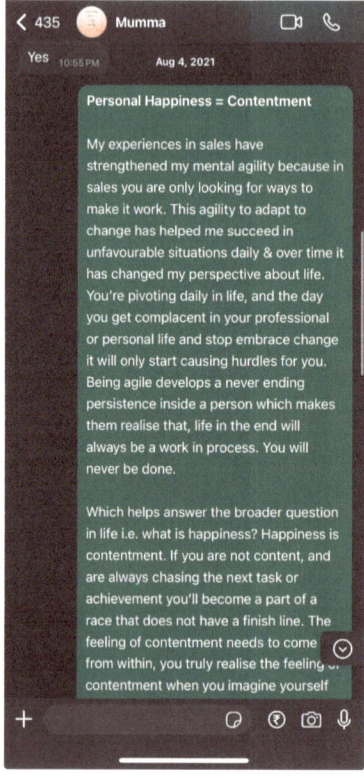

The idea came to me because ever since school, I've been chasing something. Getting admission into the university of my choice

Adaptability

(1), securing my desired major (2), landing my ideal internship (3), getting my first job (4), chasing visa sponsorship (5), and restarting my life socially {Making new friends, especially as I got older, was also a **chase.** It's not easy to build new friendships when you're older.} and professionally after moving back to India (6).

Even after figuring out my professional journey, I continued chasing. It was about finding the next big move to a financially secure future (7). Maybe that's why I found my calling in sales as a profession, I was comfortable chasing and the job entailed only chasing clients. Later, I even chased a good GMAT score (8), which always seemed elusive.

After my MBA rejection, my entrepreneurial journey began, and I've been chasing something new every day. It started with the right idea (9), finding the right partners(10), then customers(11), investors(12), employees(13), and now recurring cash flow(14). Lastly, even after losing almost 40 kgs I am still chasing my ideal weight(15).

As a guy, I chased "love" actively (16). Contrary to popular belief, love doesn't just happen; you need to make it happen. It involves a chase. And as men, society has conditioned us to make the first move, making it an experience that builds tolerance for rejection, moving on, and having lower expectations – the keys to a happy life.

I think these 16 points are enough for you to understand my point.

In **all** our lives, we're always chasing something, most centred around the things I've listed above. As we become financially well-off, we start chasing even more unnecessary things.

During these individual chases, life actually happens. If we don't pause and take some time to look back, we won't enjoy its beauty. This is when I realised that the happiest people are those who are **content** with whatever they have.

"Once I get this, I will be happy"

"Once I marry this person I will be happy"

"Once I get this job I will be happy"

If you live with the mindset of "once I achieve this, I'll be happy," you're in for disappointment.

Even though it's easier said than done for me on some days, practising gratitude rather than preaching it is always harder. You might pray to God every morning, meditate, read about mindfulness but ensuring you stick true to those learnings each hour of the day is the hardest part.

Adaptability

What helps is the skill of **adaptability.**

The internet defines it as "the quality of being able to adjust to new conditions."

Life will always put you in conditions you are not familiar with. It's imperative that you adapt to them to make the best of situations. When you actively develop this mindset, you release the unsaid pressure you've built for yourself. As you become more adaptable, situations stress you less, and you become more solution-oriented.

Example: If you didn't get your dream job, keep applying. Trust me, there's a reason why you didn't get it. If you're trying to lose weight but end up binge eating, fast the next day to lose the bloating feeling.

Very **rarely** do we get the ideal conditions for every moment in our lives. Our reactions during the hard moments are what make the conditions ideal for us.

If I hadn't been rejected from an MBA college, I wouldn't have started Build Your Own Brand (BYOB). At that moment in life either I could have folded, or gone all in. I went all in and it was because of this adaptive mindset.

Adaptive Intelligence

Our team currently :)

I enjoy binge watching shows, sharing this quote from the show Billions which cements the point I am trying to make:

"There are people to whom things happen. And there are people who make things happen. You decide who you want to be. Those who figure this out and decide to be the latter are the ones who change the world."

Adaptability

Being the latter takes conscious daily and sometimes hourly work. But once you start putting in the reps, you realise life is long and it's one adjustment after another. So being adaptable is honestly the only quality that can help you be less negative and more happy, which is literally all you need to get through to the next day and keep facing life.

Chapter 2

Rejection is Redirection

Rejection is Redirection

Rejection inherently carries a negative connotation. The word is synonymous with failure, being ignored or dismissed.

Our society has conditioned us to view rejection negatively from a young age. As soon as we can walk, we're put into a race to get into the best schools, colleges, and jobs. When we don't achieve our desired goals, we're often classified as rejected.

However, in the real world, **where** we have to earn our bread and butter, this system only works until you get into those institutions. After that, you're pretty much on your own.

Many of my role models I relate to didn't confine themselves to this traditional path. They built their fortunes through skills they learned through practice, not by getting certain percentile numbers.

Real life doesn't hit you on a predetermined date like the exam schedules we all went through.

Today's technological world of dating, where people can be rejected with a swipe without even having a chance to speak, compounds the feeling of rejection in our generation further.

All this has shaped a very negative outlook towards rejection. Unlearning this feeling or concept is an uphill task.

But my life is a **culmination** of rejections. My first big rejection was not getting my desired major at the University of Arizona, which was Architecture.

If I hadn't been rejected, I would have spent 8 years studying for a degree without any assurance of getting employment. In 2019, which is when I would have been looking for employment, it was nearly impossible for an international student to get sponsorship for architecture, due to the political environment at that time.

Because of this rejection, I ended up getting admission into the Eller College of Management. The rejection motivated me to get a higher GPA in just 2.5 semesters, leading me to a spot in the MIS program, which was the number one program at the University of Arizona in the USA in 2015.

From 2013 to 2016, I tried tirelessly to get visa sponsorship but was unsuccessful. I landed a decent internship at Bank of America in 2014 but didn't convert to a full-time role. I applied for 400+ job openings in my last year but none agreed to sponsor me. I resigned to leave the USA in 2015, but my last attempt at a job landed me an interview in Tucson, and I ended up securing it. Even then, I was always on the edge because they were only willing to keep me for 12 months. In month 10, I was told sponsorship wasn't possible, and I felt rejected yet again.

But that moment changed the course of my life.

Returning to India opened up all doors for me, and I finally could move away from tech and work in a field I felt a natural inclination for: sales.

I worked at Dineout (now Swiggy) for a year and made the biggest mistake of my professional life by deciding to leave Dineout to work at a restaurant.

However, had I not made that mistake, I wouldn't have found one of my closest friends today (Tanvi Wadhwa) or been put in a situation that forced me to figure out a way out.

I decided to cold email and reach out to Zomato, and that moment changed my life. I was able to build on my passion for sales even more deeply.

{By the way, my English teacher in high school wrote in my citation during our graduation that I had an innate ability to convince. She discovered my true calling way before I did.}

I learned how to **truly** pivot and adapt at Zomato.

My last day at the Zomato HQ in 2022

The product I joined started to change within 2 months, I reported to 10+ managers, and managed 20+ diverse individuals. I launched multiple products, some of which didn't see the light of day, but all of this still contributed to Zomato's journey. A journey that the entire country marvels at today.

The ability to let go of something you deeply loved and the concept of sunk cost is something

Rejection is Redirection

I learned at Zomato. This quality is the basis of adapting to life.

Despite multiple rejections from customers, merchants, investors, and even COVID, Zomato successfully IPO'd. If we had seen all these rejections as the end of the world, the world wouldn't be as it is today.

Towards the end of my time at Zomato, I decided to give a 100% effort to BYOB. After being rejected from ISB for not having the ideal GMAT score, I decided this was my last chance to give it all to BYOB.

From starting it as an Instagram page to showcasing it as a tech product to investors, bootstrapping it only with resume designing, and now turning it into a Personal Branding agency, all of this would not have been possible if I didn't know how to adapt.

This was our first login page in 2022

Entrepreneurship isn't just about having a kickass idea. It's about adapting until you figure out a model where your customer starts paying you recurrently.

Once you do that, all you have to do is show up daily and repeat.

The amount of rejection I've faced at BYOB is endless. From people calling it a hobby to refusing to be part of it, investors calling it unnecessary, customers signing up and ghosting, and even employees not truly buying into it.

The list is endless....

What helped me during this time was looking at these moments as learnings to build on, rather than folding in.

There are many more incidents from the 4 phases I've highlighted above during my life where I realised that we as individuals need to stop looking at rejection as something "NEGATIVE." Whatever you don't end up doing or getting as you had planned, trust me, time will tell you why it wasn't meant for you.

So whenever you feel that oh why did this relationship end?

Why did this job not work out?

Why did I exit the stock early?

You will sooner or later realise you are about to get a better and bigger opportunity in front of you.

Chapter 3

The Power of Pivot

Social media and my work environment taught me that I NEEDED to raise funds to be **considered** an entrepreneur.

However, the only quality you truly need is the ability to consistently adapt to the circumstances you're put in.

To all aspiring entrepreneurs, remember: "The idea with which you launch your business will not be the one that ends up becoming your final business."

In this chapter, I'll highlight moments where being adaptable allowed me to get this far and hopefully further.

Quick background on BYOB:

BYOB was my brainchild at the University of Arizona. It originated during my search for an internship or full-time role. I was selected for 419 interviews but couldn't get hired due to visa restrictions, while my roommates without visa restrictions were shortlisted.

That's when it clicked for me. Maybe I was good at getting shortlisted, so I started designing resumes on campus. Over the years, as I moved countries, I realised the demand for this service was pretty large. After convincing a couple of people to pay me, I gained confidence that this could be monetized.

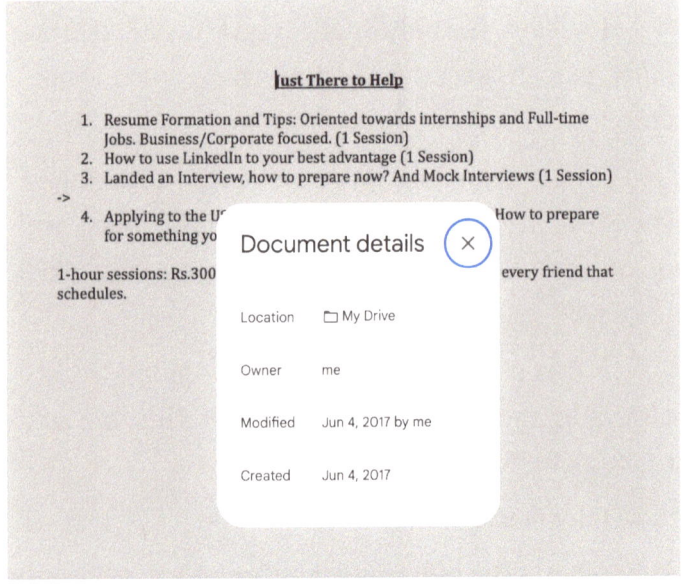

This was the first ever idea document I created for BYOB in 2017

Please note: During this time, I trademarked Build Your Own Brand and created its logo. These efforts happened between 2012 and 2018.

In 2020, I created my first few landing pages and the current Instagram page "@thebyobseries." It was a simple page where I posted 2 quotes and a story about an individual.

When I got my initial few clients and they paid what I asked for, I knew I was onto something. I pivoted towards talking to them via discovery sessions and expanded my offerings to LinkedIn, Interview Content, and Video Resume Designing.

It was during one of these initial interactions that I got the idea for our current business model of Ghostwriting. I casually suggested to one of my initial clients (a UN awardee) that they write about a specific topic on LinkedIn. She said, "This is too much effort. Would you do this for me?"

I said yes, and I knew there was a business to build here. I called this module "How to BYOB."

At that time, hand on heart, I had no clue about how to build my own brand, but I decided to wing it.

Over the next couple of months, my obsession with raising funds led me to reach out to a bunch of big names out there. After receiving responses (or none) and even meetings with some of them, I got the validation I needed.

The moment I realised I was onto something

We developed a prototype and spoke to about 30 VCs. All of them liked the idea, but no one signed the cheque.

Ironically, at this moment, I also ended up getting a job in Singapore. Honestly, it was that moment that truly pushed me to go ahead and take the leap with BYOB and go full-time. I decided to ditch the idea that funding was everything and went ahead to bootstrap the business with all my heart and money.

Within the first month, I found out that this model might not be scalable with technology or more importantly, didn't need to be scaled via technology. Personalization was key in such a service. Chasing volumes was hurting its essence.

We also discovered that people were more interested in knowing that a service that could manage their Personal Brand even existed. So I decided to double down on ghostwriting.

Before you know it, our content was published in renowned PR publications such as US Insider, NY Weekly, Economic Insider and The Emirates Times.

Lesson here: Adapt as soon as possible in your startup. Your early days are for interacting with your customers. You might think someone is your customer, but someone else might be your **ideal** customer.

Within the first year, we realised that it was much more profitable to serve 2 customers for Personal Branding than an entire batch of students for resume designing.

The next moment where I adapted was to let go of my obsession with technology. The startup ecosystem has this weird obsession with productising everything, some things DON'T need to be automated, sadly I realised this very late (or early) in our journey. After investing significant $$ into building a product that became available for cheap thanks to AI, I took the call of not being emotional with what I wanted to build and rather focus on what the customer wanted.

Lesson here: Follow the money, that's what pays the bills, not your passion. Be willing to adapt your vision, plan, and even your baby i.e. your company.

All these moments look very simple in **hindsight**. But at the moment, they take a lot of courage to execute. It's not easy to pull the plug on something you've invested heavily in financially and time-wise.

But I can promise you, I've realised that agility in adapting to change has helped me succeed in unfavourable situations. So if I could give one piece of advice, either professional or personal, it would be to be open to change, always.

The ability to adapt and pivot will make you a better entrepreneur and overall individual.

Also, the more you listen to your customers, the more customers you get, which means recurring revenue. That's what keeps any business afloat.

So develop resilience to not only take this journey but also adapt along the way. Remember to look beyond the glamour of overnight success.

It's a long-term commitment that requires you to show up daily, not just when you want to.

Chapter 4

Looking Beyond Yourself

All my life, I've struggled to find a mentor. Even today, if I had to choose, I wouldn't be able to pinpoint a single person who has been my guide or someone I can always reach out to for answers.

There were days when I felt frustrated about being in such a situation. However, over time, I used it to my advantage to strengthen my decision-making skills. I made conscious decisions myself and learned from the experiences of people around me.

As I grew older, I noticed that these people were also adapting to the circumstances life threw at them. Rather than dwelling on their situations (I don't know if they did on their own time), they were able to move on.

I realised early on that **NO ONE** has it easy. Everyone has their struggles, and it's how they react that determines their ease.

Inspiration always comes from **home** first. One incident I vividly remember from my father's career was when Enam was acquired by Axis Bank. I am sure it must have been a difficult time for him professionally, as he suddenly had to re-establish his footing in a company he was working in for decades.

My generation, when put in similar situations, might quit their jobs. But seeing my father ride out the wave through the merger showed me the benefits of sticking it out with a company. He chose to adapt in his own way.

I was put in similar situations multiple times at Zomato. Different managers, different lines of business, and tasks I didn't sign up for. But over time, I rode the wave and was rewarded for it.

My mother is the **backbone** of my family. I'll have to write a separate book for her, as I can't document her adaptive nature in just a couple of paragraphs. She adapts to the ever-changing dynamics between my dad, sister, and myself, as well as the 50+ relatives she interacts with quarterly. If someone needs to learn how to manage egos, they should reach out to her.

My point is, if you look around, you'll find **everyone** is adapting. And those we consider "successful" are always adapting.

My cousins, Rajat Kapur (Rajat Bhaiya), Bhavnidhi Kalra (Bhavnidhi Didi), Radhika Kapur (Radhika Didi), Vaibhav Kapur (Tinni Bhaiya), Pallav Kapur (Vinni Bhaiya) and Manasi Anand, have been early influencers in my life. Their careers are a combination of stability, geographic shifts, and multiple educational levels. I've looked up to them for their ability to navigate their careers and achieve financial success. While I don't know the exact number of pivots they've made, but during those pivots they always had time to indulge me 😊

My experiences with interacting with people at Communicus, Dineout, Zomato, and BYOB have taught me one thing: **no one** senior to you knows what the future holds. No one predicted the pandemic. No one knew the stock market would rise to such levels. Everyone is adapting to the current circumstances while hoping for a better tomorrow.

So the next time you lose motivation, instead of opening Instagram, just look around. You'll see everyone is in the same boat.

Chapter 5

The Power of Perspective

The Power of Perspective

We've all heard the phrase "It's all about perspective."

Implementing it in action is the hardest part. Whenever something goes unplanned or doesn't happen the way we want, we tend to be negatively affected. It takes time to find the silver lining.

However, I've observed that the silver lining always shows itself eventually. It's up to us to use it to our advantage instead of dwelling on negative thoughts and wondering about the "what if" scenarios.

Changing your perspective in situations is a great way to build adaptability. It allows you to move on from lows much faster, which is the reality of life – constantly moving from one low to another and enjoying the climb.

In this chapter, I want to highlight how I changed my perspective about returning to India after 5 years.

Like anyone who has tried to settle abroad or study abroad, they try to monetize their time there and justify an ROI to themselves. I was no different. Despite multiple efforts to get sponsorship, I was only able to get a 12-month work visa and landed back in Delhi on June 1st, 2016.

Professionally, it was the best thing that happened to me. I leveraged India's landscape, matched it with my skills, and decided to build on my circumstances rather than blaming them, even though I was making 1/10th of what I earned abroad.

If I hadn't changed my perspective about coming back to India and looking at opportunities positively, I wouldn't have found the ideal environment at Dineout and Zomato to unleash my potential and eventually launch my startup. If I kept stirring in the negativity of leaving a high paying job and blaming my circumstances, I would have ruined my mental health.

For many people, the shift from the US to India is difficult. They focus on losing personal freedom, different work environments, unprofessionalism, and lack of infrastructure.

While I agree that the quality of life is much better in the US, the tendency to feel lonely and spiral is also very high, especially if you're attached to your family and homeland.

In my last year there I lived alone without any roommates. I had the kitchen to myself, cleanliness as per my liking and everything according to me but over time what I couldn't get rid of was the loneliness feeling in my head.

I tried to fill the void by keeping the TV show Friends on in my apartment 24/7, going on trips with my cousins every weekend, and enjoying other activities. However, I realised that this lifestyle wasn't worth the money I was making.

When I moved back to India, I embraced the chaos.

Our days start with so many doorbells, chaotic traffic routes, family shenanigans, and festivals throughout the year. There's always something happening. While it can be exhausting at times, it's a blessing in disguise compared to the solitude of living abroad.

Over the last 8 years, time has flown by. Whereas in the US even after doing everything yourself, you felt time was moving slowly. I realised that having less time for yourself is actually beneficial. It prevents you from overthinking and spiralling into negativity. Especially in the social media age, which has made us even more lonely. We feel connected through messages, but our overall human connection is decreasing.

This is where my changed perspective about living in India became beneficial. Despite its challenges, India offers less time for solitude, which can be advantageous in today's world of social media isolation.

In the grand scheme of things, being able to edit, pivot, and change your perspective helps you adapt and move forward. Life will always have its ups and downs and our brain is just wired to think of lows harder than the highs, changing this behaviour helps.

Instead of being overly positive or optimistic, try to be less negative. It's a more sustainable and doable strategy to achieve better mental health.

Chapter 6

Embracing Uncertainty

Resilience is a byproduct of a **"less negative"** outlook. By changing your perspective and adapting to situations, you build resilience.

Resilience is especially crucial for entrepreneurship.

You'll notice that it often is the common theme when you read up on successful entrepreneurs.

Entrepreneurs face countless challenges. To navigate them day by day, they **need** resilience. No amount of user feedback, funding, or pivots will work if they aren't resilient.

And the only way to build resilience is to embrace change, not avoid it.

As we discussed earlier, 10% of life is what happens to you, and 90% is how you react to it.

For me, this 90% came from my experiences with rejections while looking for a job, my career in sales, trying to raise funds and convincing clients for BYOB daily.

Daily encounters with rejection built my resilience quotient to a level that not only empowered me to launch my own business but also build long-term personal relationships.

How do you look at building resilience?

The way to look at building resilience is to treat the process as a marathon or a series of short races.

These short races are testing times in your life. When you improve your ability to control your reactivity during these times, you start building resilience.

Controlling your reactions helps you remain calm and collected in the face of adversity, enabling better decision-making for your business or in your personal life.

Over time this eventually is **the** quality that your brain turns to during times of difficulty and uncertainty.

Chapter 7

The Flexible Mind

The reason we often become annoyed, irritable, reactive, or impatient is due to our obsession with controlling our surroundings, situations, and people. While it's human to feel these emotions, trying to control everything can harm ourselves.

Instead of focusing on control, we should practise the art of living and letting live. It's one of the most underrated productivity hacks.

Accepting that people change and grow is essential for maintaining relationships. Trying to control others' behaviour can lead to disappointment and even relationship breakdowns.

The art of relationship maintenance lies in balancing everyone's behaviours. It's not about completely changing yours. Eventually, everyone will get what's "good for them," not necessarily what they "wanted." i.e. the scales balance out.

There is no such thing as the ideal compatibility between 2 people, it's usually referred to romantic relationships but when you interact with your friends, family, cousins, co workers, grandparents, neighbours, I can assure you that you will never be able to say that we are 100% compatible.

The beauty of relationships lies in learning to adapt and work with incompatibility. This fosters stronger bonds, understanding, and personal growth. The idea of "soulmates" portrayed in movies and media doesn't exist in reality. We all have our quirks. We all are difficult just in different aspects.

Our false sense of belief tricks us that we can control others, actually we can only control our own actions. Trying to control someone else's behaviour will inevitably lead to disappointment.

Recently, as I planned my wedding, daily work tasks, my workout schedule, and other things, I realised that most of the time what upset me was out of my control. There is absolutely no merit in wasting one's energy in trying to control the actions of others. What we can only do is suggest something to them but we need to work very hard to not expect them to behave the way we want them to.

While implementing this we might feel we are being taken for granted, but guess what, who feels that? Only us.

By changing my perspective, I improved my mental health and became less reactive and more productive. It requires a lot of compromise and patience but by adapting to others' personalities one can create a healthy environment for everyone's growth.

Compromise often has a negative connotation, but it's the only way to create something sustainable and long-lasting. And being compromising starts with being adaptable.

Chapter 8

Navigating the Unknown

Navigating the Unknown

Not embracing the unknown and trying to subconsciously control circumstances in life can keep you in a constant state of anxiety.

When events make you think about the past or worry about the future, it can leave you feeling completely overwhelmed in the present.

What has helped me personally over the years is honing the ability to adapt through various life experiences.

The idea behind this book is to help you trace similar moments in your life and gain confidence in your own adaptability.

Those who can adapt throughout their lives are able to become the best versions of themselves. However, this best version is not a destination; it's an iterative process that never ends.

Society's artificial timelines give us a false sense of belief that we'll have everything figured out by a certain age. But the reality is, no one ever has it all figured out.

Everyone is just winging it and hoping for the best. If the outcome is favourable, they're applauded. If not, they adapt and move on.

Implementing this principle in every hour of your life will allow you to let go of your need for control and embrace the unknown. Once you do, you'll realise that life isn't so bad after all. It's just that we often obsess over things that didn't work out for us.

To overcome this, listen to the most impactful 5 seconds of the track "Tu Jhoom" by Naseebo Lal and Abida Parveen, from 1:37 to 1:42.

The lyrics, "Tere bas mein kuch vi nahi eh Dil nu eh samjhavan," mean that it's up to us to convince ourselves that our circumstances are not in our control. If you believe in a higher power (God, Karma, Fate or whatever), let it take care of things. All you have to do is dance, swirl, and let your worries fade away.

Notes Page

Jot down moments where you felt you have adapted in life

Notes Page